THE
PROMISED
ONE

Advent Readings from Christianity Today

2022

Print Managing Editor Kelli B. Trujillo
Creative Director Sarah Gordon
Senior Designer Jared Boggess
Copy Editor Alexandra Mellen

Illustration by Stephen Crotts

CONTENTS

For to us a child is born . . .

ISAIAH 9:6

During Advent, we prepare our hearts to celebrate the arrival of this child—the infant Jesus, laid in a manger, loved by Mary and Joseph, worshiped by shepherds and wise men. But Advent—which means "arrival"—invites us to prepare for much more than the holy night of his birth.

Throughout church history, Advent has been a season of antici-pation. It began in the early centuries of Christianity as a penitential period in preparation for Epiphany—the cel-ebration of Jesus' appearance and the manifestation of his identity, which was also a day set aside for the bap-tism of new believers. Soon Advent began to focus on the anticipation of another appearance: the second coming of Christ. By the Middle Ages, the themes we tend to associate with Advent today had become part of the church's observance, as Christians included celebratory anticipation of Christmas alongside their contem-plation of Jesus' return.

Each of these historical themes interweaves throughout Advent's tra-ditional Scripture readings, as the Bible's promises and prophecies speak expansively about Jesus' identity and purpose. As we delve deep into these truths, our worship of the babe in the manger is enriched, for we kneel before the one who would make his identity manifest through miracles of great power. We bow before the one who will one day come again in glory to judge the living and the dead.

The Book of Isaiah contains some of the most compelling prophecies pointing to Jesus. We read of a prom-ised son who would be called Imman-uel—God with us (7:14). We learn of a light that will dawn upon people living in darkness (9:2). And we encounter this resounding promise:

> For to us a child is born, to us a
> son is given, and the government
> will be on his shoulders. And he
> will be called Wonderful Coun-
> selor, Mighty God, Everlasting

Father, Prince of Peace. Of the greatness of his government and peace there will be no end. He will reign on David's throne and over his kingdom, establishing and upholding it with justice and righteousness from that time on and forever. (9:6–7)

Scripture's prophecies of the Promised One often have layers of meaning and multiple fulfillments. They frequently point toward a fulfillment in the prophet's own time but also direct our gaze toward the Messiah and his first coming as well as the Second Advent we await.

In this CT devotional resource, we explore what Scripture tells us about the Promised One, deepening our faith in the Savior we know and love. The daily reflections delve into key passages that help us understand more about who Jesus is. And each weekly theme centers around a core aspect of Jesus' identity drawn from Isaiah's prophecies.

THE MIGHTY GOD

The traditional first readings of Advent can feel jarringly at odds with our Christmastime expectations. Rather than holly and candlelight, we read of end-times horrors. Instead of rejoicing angels, we begin with a prophet calling loudly for repentance. These passages shock us out of our cozy mindset to remind us that Jesus is the Mighty God. The Savior whose birth we are preparing to celebrate is the very Son of Man who will one day return to judge the living and the dead. He is the one for whom God sent a messenger to prepare the way: John the Baptist, who cried out in the wilderness, testifying to Jesus' power and glory. The child in the manger is the Mighty God whose kingdom will never end.

THE PRINCE OF PEACE

Many of Advent's Old Testament passages prompt us to reflect on the personal peace we can experience with God and to envision the ultimate peace the Promised One will one day bring. War, violence, and pain will come to an end. Nations and people groups who have long been divided will worship together as one. But Scripture pushes us beyond our

tendency toward a sentimentalized vision of peace, challenging us to see that the peace Christ brings is robust and comprehensive. This peace comes not only through Jesus' love, but also through his mighty power—for his peace is tied in directly with his justice. His peace is connected to his righteous judgment. And the peace he brings was bought at a price.

THE LIGHT OF THE WORLD

From the beginning to the end of Scripture, we see light used as a metaphor to help us understand God's presence, salvation, the life of faith, and Jesus himself. We read promises of a light that would brightly shine, unhindered by darkness. When Jesus walked upon the earth, he identified himself as this promised light—the same light whose very presence will one day illuminate the city of God (Rev. 21:23). And, crucially, Jesus is the light not just for you and for me, but *for the world*. As Scripture makes plain over and over, he is the Promised One for all nations, ushering in his global, multiethnic kingdom.

IMMANUEL

This final week of Advent, we focus on the events surrounding the Nativity when the Promised One—the Mighty God, the Prince of Peace, the Light of the World—entered into humanity as a newborn child. Here was Immanuel, *God with us*. Here was the Word made flesh, dwelling among us (John 1:14). The centuries-old promises spoken about him reverberate in the acclamation of angels, the message of the shepherds, the prophetic praise of an elderly man and woman, and the joyful worship of Gentiles who'd journeyed from afar to bow before the King of Kings.

HE IS THE PROMISED ONE

This Advent, as we prepare to celebrate the birth of Jesus, may we deeply contemplate Scripture's promises of *who he is* and *what he came to do*. As we worship at the manger, may we marvel that this very child *is* the Mighty God, he *is* the Prince of Peace, and he *is* the Light of the World. He is the one who came to die. He is the one who rose triumphant, who ascended, and who will keep his promise to come again in glory. He will enact justice and bring to culmination his kingdom of peace. He is Immanuel, God with us.

The Mighty God

*The infant wrapped in swaddling clothes and laid in
a manger is the glorious Creator and sustainer of all
things. We hear of his power and might in the teachings
of John the Baptist. We anticipate his promised return
and his ultimate reign. Jesus is the Mighty God.*

Christ, the Everlasting Lord

KELLI B. TRUJILLO

For to us a child is born,
to us a son is given,
and the government
will be on his shoulders.
And he will be called
Wonderful Counselor,
Mighty God,
Everlasting Father,
Prince of Peace.
ISAIAH 9:6

O f all the common signs of this season leading up to Christmas—lights strung upon homes, Nativity scenes set out on display, trees decorated with ornaments—the one I most look forward to is the music. The songs of Advent and Christmas invite us to picture the familiar events: the holy family at the crèche, angels singing to awestruck shepherds, wise men journeying toward the "little town" of Bethlehem. These beloved hymns and carols warm our hearts.

Yet within many of our favorites are woven lyrics that break through our familiarity and declare an astonishing theological reality: The newborn in the manger *is the Mighty God.*

"Hark the Herald Angels Sing" and "We Three Kings" exhort us to comprehend who this infant truly is: "Veiled in flesh the Godhead see; hail the incarnate Deity." "Glorious now behold him arise; King and God and sacrifice."

"Come Thou Long Expected Jesus" sounds out this profound paradox in simple words: "Born a child and yet a King." These lyrics resound with the truth of Isaiah 9:6-7: This child is the Promised One who will reign eternally on David's throne, establishing his kingdom of justice, righteousness, and peace.

It's an unfathomable mystery the New Testament also invites us to dwell upon. The author of Hebrews proclaims, "The Son is the radiance of God's glory" and the "heir of all things" (1:2-3). Paul emphasizes that "in him all things were created: things in heaven and on earth, visible and invisible.... In him all things hold together" (Col. 1:16-17). Jesus Christ is supreme over all things and the fullness of God dwells in him.

This is the promised child God's people awaited and whose birth we are preparing to celebrate. This is the Lord for whom God sent a messenger to prepare the way, preaching a message of repentance. This is the Savior who, in his mission of love and redemption, would defeat the power of sin and death through his sacrifice on the cross and victorious resurrection. And this is the one whose return we await in hope, trusting in "the King of kings and Lord

of lords, who alone is immortal and who lives in unapproachable light" (1 Tim. 6:15-16).

This reality—that the child in the crèche is the Mighty God—is far beyond what we can fully comprehend. *And yet it is true.* In awe and humility, we heed the exhortation in "Oh Holy Night"—"Fall on your knees!" In humble gratitude, we worship him.

Let all within us praise his
    holy name.
Christ is the Lord! O praise
    his name forever!
His power and glory
    evermore proclaim!
His power and glory
    evermore proclaim!

Ponder Isaiah 9:6-7;
Colossians 1:15-20; and
Hebrews 1:1-12.
Optional: Also read
1 Timothy 6:13-16.

Which description of
Jesus' might and power
in these passages draws
your attention? Why? How
can this truth shape your
worship this Advent season?

Read Isaiah 40:1–5 and Malachi 3:1–4; 4:5–6

A Path Through the Wilderness

MARLENA GRAVES

A voice of one calling: "In the wilderness prepare the way for the Lord; make straight in the desert a highway for our God."

ISAIAH 40:3

In Isaiah 40, we find the Israelites deported to a strange land—exiled and captive in ancient Babylon. The city was located about an hour south of modern-day Baghdad, Iraq, and was considered the center of Mesopotamian civilization, a cosmopolitan desert city of hanging gardens that was famous for Hammurabi and his code. But God's people didn't want to remain stranded here. They wanted to go *home*, back to Jerusalem. Yet they were far, far away from home with no hope of return.

In this no-hope-possible context, they experienced an inbreaking of God's grace. "Comfort," the prophet cried—a Hebrew word with connotations of *courage* and *strength*. His message was something akin to "Be comforted, have hope! This is not the end. You are going to see and experience something you could never have imagined in your wilderness life." Like their ancient ancestors who had experienced miraculous provision and deliverance in the Egyptian wilderness, they too would see God make a path through the wilderness for them.

Pairing Isaiah 40:1–5 with Malachi 3:1–4 and 4:5–6, we see God's promise to send a messenger to prepare the hearts of his people for deliverance. They would be cleansed as through fire so that they might see God, themselves, and the world more clearly. In this deliverance, that which had been torn apart through exile, like familial relationships, would one day be stitched back together (Mal. 4:5–6).

God kept his word; eventually the Israelites returned to Jerusalem. Yet this return was not the end of the prophecy. Centuries later, another prophet, John the Baptist, would clear the path for the Mighty God, our Lord Jesus Christ, to save his people from their exilic existence—exiled from God and one another due to sin. John would soften people's hearts for Christ's arrival.

And there is another layer of fulfillment of Malachi's prophecy (3:1–4): It points toward Jesus' second coming when we will be refined—made pure—as all things are made new (see Rev. 21:5).

Fantastic deliverances in hopeless situations are not relegated to ancient history. Almighty God pulls off spectacular feats of deliverance daily. Indeed, God appears when all hope seems lost. We can trust in the mightiness of God. And, during Advent, we're reminded to trust the Promised One who came to us as a newborn babe yet held all the power and might of the universe and beyond in his tiny hands!

Are you in the wilderness in need of deliverance—in need of God in his might to intervene? We may not know how or when deliverance may come, but *it will come*. God always comes. Ask God to prepare your heart for his arrival and the deliverance that always comes with it.

Contemplate Isaiah 40:1–5 and Malachi 3:1–4; 4:5–6.

How do you see God's might in these promises? In their layers of fulfillment? How do these passages resonate with your own longings and desires?

True Cleansing

MADISON N. PIERCE

I baptize you with water for repentance. But after me comes one who is more powerful than I, whose sandals I am not worthy to carry. He will baptize you with the Holy Spirit and fire.

MATTHEW 3:11

If we're honest, at first glance John the Baptist is about the worst hype man you could imagine. He's dressed in a belted hair shirt and eats locusts. As he comes into the wilderness of Judea, he begins to preach. We could certainly imagine a proclamation of the coming Messiah that would tickle the ears a bit more. He could remind people of the great promises associated with the Messiah—that the Messiah will bring justice, provide healing, offer stability. He could tell them the *good news*.

John, however, does something quite different. He says, "Repent, for the kingdom of heaven has come near," and through Matthew's use of the quotation from Isaiah 40:3, we see that John tells the people with familiar and authoritative words to "make straight their paths"—or "straighten up" (see also John 1:23). John starts with what might be considered the bad news, really; he tells them that they need to change.

And many of them listen. How is this strange man so successful in ministry? Matthew gives us hints. He offers a selective description of John, and each detail is loaded with significance. His hair shirt with a leather belt? The attire of Elijah. His locusts and honey? The meal of the poor. Matthew presents this man in the style of the prophets of old, as an authoritative man of God who declares the word of the Lord.

The people approach John for cleansing—ritual washing that symbolizes their repentance—but he promises that more effective cleansing is coming. This cleansing from the Lord will come via "the Holy Spirit and fire."

As John continues to explain the ministry of the coming one, his metaphors help us understand what it means to be baptized in Spirit and fire. It is purification (in part) through separating out what is good from what is bad. John uses the agricultural metaphor we see in places like Psalm 1, a process well known to his audience. Farmers would use a winnowing fork to throw grain in the air. The heavy, edible parts would fall to the ground, but the chaff was lighter and generally would blow away. If any extra chaff was left over after this, the farmer would separate it out and burn it.

This is a more permanent cleansing than a washing, and I think that's precisely the point. The people's baptism by John is significant, but without the accompanying work of the Spirit, its effects are temporary. With just the baptism of John, they will need to wash again, but the work of Jesus through the Spirit is effective for all time.

Reflect on Matthew 3:1-12.

How would you describe John's message? Why is it good news? In prayer, consider what John's words emphasize about Jesus' power and purpose.

Read John 1:19–34 and 3:22–30

Jesus Deserves All the Attention

CRAIG L. BLOMBERG

He must become greater; I must become less.

JOHN 3:30

H e must increase, but I must decrease" (KJV). I remember hearing this verse as a child and imagining Jesus growing bigger and bigger while John the Baptist shrank! The context of John's statement clarifies his meaning: John's disciples have told him that "everyone is going" to Jesus, so John declares, "He must become greater; I must become less."

John's ministry began before Jesus' did, so John watched the number of Jesus' followers grow from zero to a lot more than John had. This could have been heartbreaking, because "the whole Judean countryside and all the people of Jerusalem" had been going out to the wilderness to see John (Mark 1:5).

The Gospel of John, however, consistently depicts John the Baptist merely as a witness—one who bears

testimony—to the identity and greatness of Jesus. Each portion of today's two passages shows John explaining who he is and isn't or who Jesus is. Jewish leaders from Jerusalem question John about his identity, and he denies being any kind of Messiah. He is just preparing the way for the Christ. Yes, he has a ministry of water baptism, but his status is greatly inferior to that of the coming one. John points out Jesus as God's sacrificial lamb, who will take away the sins of the world, and who will immerse people into the power of the Holy Spirit.

Later, when Jesus' followers have eclipsed John's in number, John insists this is fully appropriate. He likens himself simply to the best man in a wedding, where Jesus is the groom. John's analogy in 3:29 is striking, particularly when we understand its cultural context. Ancient Jewish custom called for the best man to wait outside the bedroom when the bride and groom consummated the marriage. Traditionally, the groom would shout for joy to confirm their new marital intimacy, and the best man would share that joy.

The Christian life is all about deferring more and more to Jesus, the Mighty God. A generation later, Paul would say in Philippians 1:18 that "the important thing is that in every way... Christ is preached. And because of this I rejoice."

I have recently retired and need to learn this lesson more than ever. Being in the limelight is not the point. Humbly magnifying Jesus is. I need to shrink.

Meditate on John 1:19-34 and 3:22-30.

Consider what John the Baptist's example shows us about who Jesus is. How is John's posture instructive for your own spiritual life? How might you "become less"?

Jesus Will Reign

CRAIG L. BLOMBERG

So you also must be ready, because the Son of Man will come at an hour when you do not expect him.

MATTHEW 24:44

Q uestions arise with the first word of this passage: "Immediately"!

Most of the rest of the content in verses 29–31 has almost always been understood to describe Christ's return, depicted poetically in the language of Isaiah 13:10 and 34:4 as involving cosmic upheaval. (Some have instead taken it as a sort of invisible coming of Jesus in judgment through Rome's destruction of Jerusalem in A.D. 70—though the idea of gathering the elect from one corner of the world to another doesn't fit that interpretation.)

When will Christ come back? This message on the Mount of Olives was provoked by Jesus' disciples asking him when he would come back (Matt. 24:3). He itemized a long list of what must happen first (vv. 4–26) and now says, in essence, "Watch for these things to know when my coming is near," just as a fig tree in leaf portends the arrival of summer.

Examples of all "these things" occurred by A.D. 70, so the church in every generation since has believed it might see his return. Jesus is not saying he will return in the disciples' lifetime, merely that all the preparatory events will have occurred. "These things" in verse 34 have to be the same as "these things" in verse 33—which show that Christ's return "is near" but not yet here. So they can't include his actual return—just the signs that prepared for his return. When he returns, he will no longer be merely "near, right at the door," but he will have arrived! We can't know the precise timing of all this, so we must always be prepared. Those who aren't will be caught off guard by the suddenness and surprise of the final events. If we remain alert at all times, we don't have to worry about a midnight burglar. Of course, Jesus isn't coming back to steal anything from us; it is the idea of *unexpectedness* he's highlighting in this comparison.

But what about "immediately after the distress of those days"? Perhaps the distress here is the distress that characterizes the entire period between Christ's two comings. After all, 2 Timothy 3:12 promises persecution to all the godly (even amid the many joyous moments in the Christian life).

However we interpret it, here is testimony to Jesus as the Mighty God who will put all things right in his perfect timing. Today, many Christians have recovered the biblical call for justice in this life, and rightly so—we should do all we can to help others. But war, sickness, natural disaster, injury and disability, poverty, and broken relationships all require us to ultimately trust God for *complete* restitution and restoration in eternity.

Contemplate
Matthew 24:29-44.

What questions does this passage raise for you? What feelings does it stir up? Pray, reflecting on how it points your focus toward Jesus' might and power.

The Judge Who Is Faithful & True

GLENN PACKIAM

I saw heaven standing open and there before me was a white horse, whose rider is called Faithful and True. With justice he judges and wages war.

REVELATION 19:11

T he grad student dialoguing with me was heavy with questions posed by her agnostic friends about hell and God's judgment. She found it hard to reconcile the God of love and the message of forgiveness with visions of fiery torment. As we talked, I explained that there are many orthodox Christian views of what the final judgment will be like, but the *main* thing Christians are asked to do is to trust Jesus as the Judge. She was visibly relieved.

For whatever reason—we might blame Dante or folk religion or medieval superstition—we often imagine God's judgment to be impersonal and cold, like a mass execution or a bomb detonated from a distance. But Revelation deliberately shows us *Jesus* involved in the judgment of the nations. I think there are two reasons for this.

First, justice and judgment are two sides of the same coin. To enact justice, one must execute judgment. If we want Jesus the Mighty God to set the world right, he must deal with injustice and evil together. Here the justice and judgment of Jesus are depicted in a vivid way that would have held sway in first-century minds: a warrior on a horse with a sword. But we must be careful with our assumptions here.

Which leads us to the second reason why Jesus is shown as the one who carries out justice and judgment: The Jesus who is returning is the same Jesus who came. *There is no change of identity between advents.* "Jesus Christ is the same yesterday and today and forever" (Heb. 13:8); this conviction helps us consider *how* Jesus enacts justice and executes judgment. On the cross, Jesus died in solidarity with the sinner and the sufferer. He bore the weight of God's judgment on evil.

If we were to ask how Jesus responds to injustice and evil, the answer is *he bleeds.* Judgment fell on him so that justice—wrongs being set right—could come to all. When we see Jesus coming like a warrior whose robe is dipped in blood, the blood could well be his own. After all, this is a king like none other. Jesus embodies might and power in a way we've never known before.

Yet this passage doesn't leave us without a warning. There are those who resist this king, who insist on their own way, their own rule, their own empire. For them, life will meet its end. The gruesome images of being devoured depict the erosion of life. The King of Kings brings life by his death. But if you resist his life and insist on protecting your own, instead of life you will get death.

Judgment and justice belong together. And the one who will carry out both is Faithful and True. Will we trust him with enacting justice and executing judgment?

Consider Revelation 19:4–21.

How can your knowledge of Jesus and his first advent speak into your understanding of the Second Advent? Of the justice and judgment of the King of Kings?

The Greatest Hope of All

GLENN PACKIAM

I magine a boy being bullied on the playground. Kids surround him, taunt him, push him onto the ground. He's fighting back the tears, but that's about all he can fight; there's no way to stop the terror and the torment.

Then, almost out of nowhere, a car pulls up. It's the kid's father. "Get in the car, son," the dad yells. Rolling out of the other kids' grasp, the boy scrambles to his feet and stumbles to the car. They speed off. As the boy looks briefly out the window, he is sure the bullies are laughing. The boy is safe, but there's no way to count that as a win. An evacuation is not a victory.

The end of the Book of Revelation—the end of the Bible itself—shows us a picture not of our evacuation or escape but of God's arrival. Jesus conquered sin and death on the cross. In John's gospel, Jesus said from the cross, "It is finished" (19:30). Here, in John's revelation, the one who is seated on the throne says, "It is done." The first statement was an announcement of completion; the second is a proclamation of things coming to pass. The victory of Jesus on the cross was made manifest in his resurrection, but it will arrive in fullness at his return.

We know that the season of Advent is a time of waiting between two arrivals. But the truth is, it is also a waiting between two *victories*. Jesus the Mighty One has overcome, and Jesus the Mighty One is coming again.

And when he comes, he comes to *dwell*. The vision of the end that Revelation provides is of God making heaven and earth new, uniting the new heaven and the new earth as one, and filling it with his presence

And I heard a loud voice from the throne saying, "Look! God's dwelling place is now among the people, and he will dwell with them. They will be his people, and God himself will be with them and be their God."

REVELATION 21:3

and light. This is a victory that comes with an occupation—only in this case, the occupation is good news, the best news the world could receive! The Creator has redeemed his creation and has come to fill it with his glory. The story that began in Genesis has been perfected and completed.

Back to the playground. Creatively imagine a totally different scenario: Instead of the dad yelling for his kid to get in so they can drive away, the dad parks the car, gets out, and walks slowly over. The authority of his very presence drives away the bullies. He embraces his son. He calls out to other kids who are hiding, who are hurting, to come out into the light. He decides to settle in and remake the playground entirely, now with better equipment and brighter delights. Food and drinks arrive. Then comes the music. And ice cream. Laughter abounds. Somehow the place of pain has become the place of joy.

Reflect on Revelation 21:1–6 and 21:22–22:5.

What stands out to you in this description of the Mighty One's ultimate reign? What hope and comfort does it bring? How do you desire to respond to Jesus?

The Prince of Peace

*Amid the pain and violence of our world, we hold fast to
this hope: One day Jesus will usher in true and ultimate
peace. He also brings us spiritual peace in the here
and now as we experience redemption and live by the
values of his kingdom. Jesus is the Prince of Peace.*

A Vision of Peace

CAROLYN ARENDS

Nation will not take up sword against nation, nor will they train for war anymore.

ISAIAH 2:4

P erhaps the greatest evidence that the Promised One is the Mighty God is this: He is the one—the *only* one—with a power great enough to bring lasting peace. He not only brings peace, he *is* peace. The Prince of Peace.

We are, of course, accustomed to a world in which peace is maddeningly elusive. In 2003, journalist Chris Hedges set out to determine whether there have been any sustained periods of peace on the human record. Defining *war* as any "active conflict that has claimed more than 1,000 lives," he reviewed 3,400 years of history and discovered just 268 war-free years. In other words, approximately 92 percent of recorded history is marked by active conflict.

Of course, the people of ancient Israel did not need a journalist to tell them that human existence is plagued by wars and rumors of wars. They had

plenty of firsthand, trauma-inducing experience with conflict, violence, and oppression. What they *did* need was a prophet who could provide them with a vision of peace vivid enough to counter the horrific images already seared into their memories.

Isaiah brought them—and us—just such a vision. Consider the images in the second chapter of Isaiah. All the nations come streaming together to the mountain of God. That's where they discover that the supposed dichotomy between peace and justice has been false all along. The Lord brings peace *through* justice. He judges between the nations and settles disputes, resolving not only wars but also their underlying causes.

And then watch what happens when humans find themselves in the presence of the Prince of Peace: The swords and spears they've brought to the mountain—weapons they've long assumed were necessary to their survival—seem suddenly out of place. The people lay down their arms. But the Prince of Peace has something even more beautiful in mind. Soon, the people are working together to convert their weapons into gardening tools. Human ingenuity is redeemed and redirected from destructive ends to creative ends.

Isaiah is not naive. He has seen the brutality that can and does characterize the human condition. But he's also caught a glimpse of the verdant, vibrant, peace-infused future the Prince of Peace has planned for his creation. It's the sort of vision that gives a weary prophet hope—a vision about the sort of prince who will one day cause angels to exclaim, "Glory to God in the highest heaven, and on earth peace to those on whom his favor rests" (Luke 2:14).

Meditate on Isaiah 2:1-5 and 9:6-7.

What most strikes you about Isaiah's vision of peace? How does this hope speak into our world today? Pray, expressing praise to the promised Prince of Peace.

The Prince of Shalom

CAROLYN ARENDS

Water will gush forth in the wilderness and streams in the desert.

ISAIAH 35:6

T he Hebrew word that Isaiah uses to describe the peace that the Promised One will bring is *shalom*. It's a beautiful word that conveys wholeness, harmony, and health. Where we might settle for uneasy truces and Band-Aid fixes as proxies for peace, shalom represents something much more robust. Beyond the cessation of war, shalom is a transformation of the conditions that lead to war in the first place.

When there is shalom, everything gets to function the way it was created to. Shalom rejects the idea of life as a zero-sum game and dares to imagine the comprehensive flourishing of every person and every thing, all at the same time. Theologian Darrell Johnson teaches that *shalom* describes "a psycho-somatic-relational-racial-economic-spiritual wholeness." In chapter 35, Isaiah depicts that wholeness in beautifully poetic language. Let's start with the psychological wholeness the Prince of Shalom can offer us. According to Isaiah, there is a peace on offer that says, "Be strong, do not fear" to our "fearful hearts" (v. 4) until "gladness and joy" overtake us and "sorrow and sighing... flee away" (v. 10).

And what of somatic (or bodily) wholeness? In one vivid image after an another, Isaiah describes physical healing: The blind see, the deaf hear, the lame "leap like a deer" and the mute "shout for joy" (vv. 5–6). Even the creation itself is healed, as "water will gush forth in the wilderness" (v. 6) and "the wilderness will rejoice and blossom" like a crocus flower bursting into bloom (vv. 1–2).

As Isaiah 35 builds to its culmination, we are offered a vibrant vision of relational, economic, and spiritual wholeness in the depiction of a redeemed people walking and singing together on a highway of holiness. There are no lions there, Isaiah tells us, and we can safely assume the way is free from all other predatory or opportunistic foes. The people enter Zion together, where "everlasting joy will crown their heads" (v. 10).

This ultimate shalom, Isaiah tells us, is our future. But there's even more to it than that. Author Jonathan Martin suggests in *Prototype* that, because the Prince of Peace gives us his Spirit, we are called to be "people from the future"—people who practice shalom here and now.

This Advent, when you face a situation in which peace is sorely needed, ask the Lord: *What action or attitude would most move this situation toward the comprehensive flourishing of everyone and everything involved?* You may find that the Prince of Shalom makes *you* a stream in the desert and fills you with gladness and joy.

Contemplate Isaiah 35.

What words or phrases would you use to describe the peace envisioned here? How does it speak to our future hope? How does it speak to the work of the Prince of Peace in our lives today?

Peaceful Rest

ADRIEL SANCHEZ

In that day the Root of Jesse will stand as a banner for the peoples; the nations will rally to him, and his resting place will be glorious.

ISAIAH 11:10

One of the great tensions we often feel during Advent is the disparity between God's promise of peace and the presence of war and violence in our world. Isaiah foretold that the Messiah's reign would bring a world without worry. Picture a mother at perfect rest, watching her children play by the cobra's den and not leaping into action. As a father of five, I find this is hard to imagine!

Parents know that feeling of overwhelming panic when their child approaches danger. During the Messiah's reign, as Isaiah describes it, that feeling will go extinct.

But in our lived experience, the world doesn't look anything like this. Thomas Hardy's nearly 100-year-old poem "Christmas: 1924" laments,

"Peace upon earth!" was said.
We sing it,
And pay a million priests to
bring it.
After two thousand years of mass
We've got as far as poison-gas.

How do we reconcile the promise of peaceful rest with the reality of poison gas—or ballistic missiles? The answer lies in the tension of the *now and not yet*. During Isaiah's day, the promises God had made to King David in 2 Samuel 7—promises of an enduring and blessed kingdom—seemed broken. The house of David resembled a felled tree. But from its dry stump a Spirit-filled branch would emerge: Jesus, the Son of David. He would bring peace to both Jews and Gentiles, standing as a rallying flag to unite hostile nations (Isa. 11:10; Eph. 2:15).

This is realized *now* in part through the church, where even tax collectors like Levi and zealots like Simon find peace through Christ's blood. God's worldwide temple is made of living stones, and the bricks God builds with are chosen from every tribe, tongue, and nation. Today we can experience the promised peace of the messiah-king who says to the weary, "I will give you rest" (Matt. 11:28).

But the *not yet* of Isaiah's prophecy will arrive with Jesus' second advent (Isa. 11:4; 2 Thess. 2:8). This is anticipated by the Edenic imagery of subdued predatory animals in Isaiah's prophecy. Jesus will one day perfectly subdue creation, calming deadly beasts and turning even a serpent into a child's plaything. The glorified world of the new creation will ultimately satisfy our deepest longings for justice and peace.

Advent reminds us of the glorious rest given through Jesus's first coming and anticipates the full restoration that will accompany his return. In this time of tension—between the now and not yet—God calls us to be marked by his kingdom grace, a people who pursue justice for the oppressed and spread the knowledge of Christ in our communities (Isa. 11:9; 2 Cor. 2:14). It is through this knowledge that weary sinners receive the glorious rest of Christ's kingdom.

Ponder Isaiah 11:1–10.

Which descriptions of peace most draw your attention? Why? Pray, expressing your longing for the peace Christ brings in the now—and in the not yet.

The Healing Peace of Jesus

BETH STOVELL

*A bruised reed
he will not break,
and a smoldering
wick he will not
snuff out.*

ISAIAH 42:3

I saiah and Matthew knew what it means that Jesus is the Prince of Peace. When Matthew described Jesus as fulfilling Isaiah 42:1–4, we see an image of *shalom*, the Hebrew word for *peace*. Unlike our often narrow understanding of peace as simply being "without war," shalom encompasses a broad picture of how God makes everything wrong with the world *right*. This shalom of God is a peace that brings order out of chaos and justice in place of injustice.

Isaiah 42 starts by introducing God's chosen one, "my servant." This is the first of what some call the Servant Songs; the other songs are found in 49:1–6, 50:4–9, and 52:13–53:12. They tell a story of God's servant enacting salvation to the ends of the earth (in chapters 42, 49, 50) and saving God's people through the servant's own suffering (in 52–53).

Here, in 42:1–4, the servant is the one God holds up and delights in. This

servant brings God joy! God's Spirit is on this servant, so that he can bring justice to the nations. This isn't a message of peace only for Israel, but for the whole world.

One might expect this Spirit-filled servant to be loud and proud about his chosen status with God, but instead he is characterized by his humility. He's not shouting out in the streets, but instead he's caring for those who are hurting. He's someone who can see that a reed is bruised—that a person is feeling trampled—but he won't let them break. He's someone who holds a person who feels like a tiny candle on the verge of going out, and he won't let their light fade. What does it mean to bring peace to those who are barely hanging on? The servant's quest for justice is characterized by gentleness. He sees those experiencing vulnerability; he won't let them fall.

Matthew 12 describes how Jesus fulfills Isaiah's prophecy. It may look at first like Jesus is fulfilling this prophecy by asking his disciples to keep quiet (v. 16), similar to the quiet of the servant in Isaiah 42. But if we look at the entire chapter, Matthew shows us something different. Jesus, as the servant, cares for those who need healing. In the passages before and after verses 15–21, the emphasis is on how Jesus healed on the Sabbath (vv. 1–14), how Jesus "healed all who were ill" (v. 15), and how he healed a demon-possessed man, bringing him sight and the ability to speak (v. 22).

Jesus' kind of peace meets us in our weakest places, transforming injustice into justice, setting right what has been bruised, and he does this with the gentleness of his loving touch.

Reflect on Isaiah 42:1-4 and Matthew 12:15-21. *Optional: Also read Matthew 12:1-14, 22-37.*

How have you experienced the shalom of Jesus that Isaiah and Matthew describe? What other scenes in the Gospels come to mind as examples of Jesus' peace?

Our Jubilean Hope

SARAH SHIN

*He has sent me
to bind up the
brokenhearted, to
proclaim freedom
for the captives and
release from darkness
for the prisoners, to
proclaim the year of
the Lord's favor.*

ISAIAH 61:1-2

When Jesus unfurled the scroll and read Isaiah 61, his hearers had been waiting for many generations for the Promised One—the Prince of Peace, the bringer of justice and freedom. They'd seen countless wars, successive occupying empires, and cultural changes that disoriented them as they navigated having faith in such circumstances.

We too live in times of geopolitical chaos, violence, and confusion. We too wait for the Prince of Peace to come in glory, to bring the final resurrection and restoration to places of death and mourning. It hurts to wait. It fills us with longing.

Isaiah 61:1-4 refers to the Jubilee Year in Leviticus 25—a radical command that called for restoring land and people who had been sold into

slavery because of debt. The Jubilee Year was the year of the Lord's favor, when debt-slaves would be freed and homes and lands would be restored. God desired every daughter and son of Israel to be restored to *home*. Yet Isaiah 61 also speaks of God's vengeance—and Jesus unsettlingly says that he has come to bring not peace but the sword and division (Matt. 10:34–36). How then, could Jesus be the bringer of peace?

When Isaiah speaks of the Prince of Peace, he's speaking of shalom— which is not only the absence of violence or evil, but also the fullness of a good life—of loving one's neighbor to see her flourishing and following a loving God each day.

The weekly Sabbath breaks our rhythms of work with rest and shalom, and the Jubilee is the Sabbath of Sabbaths. It is the *pinnacle* of shalom. So when Jesus declares the arrival of jubilean shalom, he not only offers salvation from judgment after this life but also asserts that *he* is the arrival of deliverance from slavery to both monetary and spiritual debt—into freedom and restoration in this life and beyond.

Thus, Jesus' birth and life are more than a prelude to the Cross. Indeed, his birth, his life, the Cross, and the Resurrection are all part of the larger story of God delivering his people—

a people who trust God and love their neighbor. As the Israelites were called to trust in God for deliverance and provision in the wilderness, so we are called to lean upon the Lord for the same—against all odds and in war, political turmoil, or wandering. And we're called to love our neighbor as part of that active hope.

Jesus inaugurated the Jubilee in the shadow of the occupying Roman Empire, and he invites us, despite the shadows all around, to follow him and to live in his jubilean kingdom. He bids us to actively yearn, hope, and wait for his resurrection power to break through in unexpected ways as he moves and lives in us.

Consider Isaiah 61:1-4 and Luke 4:16-21. *Optional: Also read Leviticus 25.*

How does the idea of Jubilee enrich your reading of Isaiah's prophecy? Of Jesus identifying himself as its fulfillment? Of Jesus as the Prince of Peace?

Born to Be Bruised

ALICIA AKINS

He was pierced for our transgressions, he was crushed for our iniquities; the punishment that brought us peace was on him, and by his wounds we are healed.

ISAIAH 53:5

E xpectation mounted as God's people awaited their Messiah's arrival, just as we now await the celebration of his birth. Yet this fourth Servant Song in Isaiah reads much more like a eulogy than a birth announcement. It speaks of one who is not just coming, but of one who is *sent*. Each part of the servant's biography is imbued with purpose.

The servant's story is no mere tragedy. On the contrary, this song begins and ends by affirming the promised servant's triumph and exaltation. The middle of the song fleshes out *how* he will succeed: through suffering. Physically, the servant would be marred, pierced, crushed, and disfigured. Emotionally, his soul would be weighed down with sorrow, suffering, and anguish. Socially, he would be rejected, despised, and oppressed. His body, spirit, and relationships would be broken. This inestimable yet unenviable life would be cut short, undervalued, and profaned. "Yet," Isaiah says, "it was the Lord's will to crush him and cause him to suffer." But why? For what purpose? Because "the punishment that brought us peace was on him." His sorrow-sunk shoulders would carry the grief of the world, his crushing would remove our guilt, his welts would secure our healing, and his ostracization and judgment would purchase our peace. As messianic prophecies, these songs point to a set-apart king-priest who would one day rule and make offerings for God's people. In the New Testament, both Philip and Peter see Christ as this song's fulfillment. Philip explains the gospel to the Ethiopian eunuch using this passage (Acts 8:26–40). Peter uses this song to exhort persecuted Christ-followers to endure because their path of suffering was well trod by their Savior (1 Pet. 2:22–24).

As we reflect on Jesus as the Prince of Peace, this passage challenges the tranquil and idyllic images of peace we may conjure up in our minds. Our peace was won through gruesome violence against Jesus—it cost him a lifetime punctuated by sorrow, being misunderstood, and rejection. This suffering is what awaited the peace-bringing baby of our carols.

Our image of the Christ child swaddled and held tenderly by his parents contrasts sharply with the difficult truth of this Servant Song—of the Father not only sending the Son to an early death, but purposing it. While most human parents hope and pray for bright futures for their children, here we see a love-driven death mission that will secure the survival of many. This song doesn't only tell us about the servant sent to suffer, but also of the Father's heart: eager to save his people at any expense, even at the gravest personal cost.

Contemplate
Isaiah 52:13–53:12.
Optional: Also read the third Servant Song in Isaiah 50:4–9.

———————————

How does the suffering described here contrast with your vision of peace? How does it change or enrich it?

Jesus Is Our Peace

KELLY M. KAPIC

T wo truths can be in conflict, and yet if they *are* true, we need to affirm them both.

First, our world is filled with genuine pain and trouble. As the Old Testament prophets warned, our rebellion against God has twisted us and our world. To pretend otherwise is to be naive at best or hard-hearted at worst. God doesn't ask us to lie about the hardships of life.

Second, Jesus is our peace—not in a cheap or cheesy way but in an earthy, knowing, cosmos-altering way. He is the only answer to this pain and trouble. Sent by the Father in the power of the Spirit, the Son of God became fully and truly human. This God of peace breaks into our broken world as one of us and starts a renewed world, realizing the ancient prophetic hope. "He himself is our peace," since "in his flesh" he breaks down the "dividing wall of hostility"—not just between the sinner and God, but also between Jew and Gentile, male and female, rich and poor, heaven and earth (Gal. 3:28; Col. 1:15–22).

And these two truths clash.

Jesus is our peace, not merely in some psychological manner, but also in a concrete, whole-life way. He is our peace, not by numbing us, but by forgiving and healing us and enfolding us into in his love and life. Even in the darkness of night and when confusion, doubt, and chaos swirl, Jesus still says, "Do not let your hearts be

*For he himself
is our peace.*

EPHESIANS 2:14

troubled and do not be afraid," and "Peace I leave you; my peace I give you" (John 14:27).

We recognize trouble and brokenness as painful and problematic because they don't resemble shalom. Whereas shalom brings harmony, goodness, and a flourishing world, we live amid wars, betrayal, and our own suffocating self-absorption. But in response to our rebellion and chaos Jesus brings his peace, his shalom. "I have told you these things, so that in me you may have peace. . . . Take heart! I have overcome the world" (John 16:33). By connecting us to God, *he* is our shalom. *He* is Israel's hope and thus the hope of the world.

This is how we have peace in a genuinely troubled world: God, from beyond our world, has given us himself as our peace. Christ, the God-man, is our peace: He doesn't depend on our fluctuating emotions and circumstances. God doesn't ask us to lie about pain and problems or about his goodness and presence in Christ. Both are true. Beloved, there is trouble, but Christ is our peace amid trouble, and he gives us refuge, strength, and direction to extend his peace to this hurting world.

Meditate on
John 14:27; 16:33; and Ephesians 2:14–18.

How is Jesus your peace in a concrete, whole-life way—even amid the very real hardships of life?

The Light of the World

Scripture uses the motif of darkness and light to
describe the Promised One—and Jesus identified
himself as this prophesied light. In him, we experience
salvation and spiritual illumination. But Jesus is
not only the light for us as individuals—he is a light
for all nations. Jesus is the Light of the World.

A Light Has Dawned

JEREMY TREAT

The people walking in darkness have seen a great light; on those living in the land of deep darkness a light has dawned.

ISAIAH 9:2

G rowing up in a small town in Alaska, I was well acquainted with darkness. In the depths of the winter, a mere few hours of sunlight each day would quickly give way to the long, unforgiving nights. And the effects of the darkness went beyond the inconvenience of shoveling the driveway under artificial light. The lack of light brought about a lack of hope. The long winters of Alaska produce isolation, depression, and sometimes despair. In the darkness, there is no vision, no direction, and no purpose.

Isaiah 8 tells of a time when Israel was well acquainted with darkness. Under the threat of invasion by an international superpower (Assyria), God's people were in a place of fear and dread. Rather than turning to God as their hope, they doubled down on their fear by embracing conspiracies and consulting with occultic mediums (vv. 12, 19), which led them only deeper into utter darkness.

And yet, amid this distress, the prophet Isaiah proclaims that "the people walking in darkness have seen a great light." Despite their own attempts to claw their way out of the darkness, a light has dawned upon them. What is this light? Who could bring hope amid utter darkness? Isaiah declares, "For to us a child is born."

While a child is certainly no match for the Assyrian military, *this* child is different. This son will grow up to be a king who will rule with righteousness and justice. Though he will reign from David's throne, his kingdom will extend to the ends of the earth and will be established for all of eternity. Through this anointed child, not only will the light shine amid the darkness, but the light will *overcome* it.

The promise given by Isaiah was ultimately fulfilled hundreds of years later when a child, a son, was born under the threat of another international superpower. Jesus is the Light of the World. And while our world still remains in utter gloom, the light of the gospel shines bright amid the darkness. For this king reigns with grace and rules with love. Of his kingdom, there will be no end.

The winters in Alaska were harsh. But I have not told you about the summers. At the height of summer in Alaska, there is daylight 24 hours a day. *No darkness. All light. So much joy.* When Christ returns, he will make all things new. And the Book of Revelation tells us that in the new creation, there will be no need for the sun (22:5), for the glory of God will shine brighter than a thousand suns! We will walk in the light and experience the pure joy of Christ's kingdom forevermore.

Consider Isaiah 8:21–9:7.

How does the historical context of this great promise impact your understanding? How does it speak into our context today?

Salvation and Love

BETH STOVELL

*I, the Lord, have
called you in
righteousness;
I will take hold of
your hand. I will
keep you and will
make you to be a
covenant for the
people and a light
for the Gentiles.*

ISAIAH 42:6

W e have all experienced what it is like to wake up in darkness—that moment when we are grasping for the light so that we can see the world around us clearly. Perhaps like me, you never fully grew out of that fear of the dark. Darkness is a universal fear because it can create spaces of danger, whereas light guides us toward safety. Especially before the invention of electric lights, darkness meant that a person was more likely to experience an attack by enemies or dangerous animals.

It should not surprise us, then, that light is a powerful metaphor for safety and salvation in Isaiah as he describes God's servant fulfilling this role. We see this idea in the New Testament as Jesus is described as the "light of the world" (John 8:12; 9:5), echoing the descriptions of God's servant as the light of salvation for the whole world in Isaiah 42, 49, and 60.

Isaiah places two ideas next to one another as he pictures God's servant: God's global salvation and God's deep intimacy. On the one hand, the servant will bring salvation on a global scale. Like the light of the sun that reaches across the earth from end to end, God's servant will bring salvation to all people, every tribe, every nation (42:6; 49:6; 60:3). This salvation is multiethnic, multicultural, and available for all.

On the other hand, when Isaiah depicts this salvation—the servant's global light—he also anchors this vast vision in God's deep intimacy. This God formed the servant within his mother's womb (49:5), labors like a woman giving birth for his people's salvation (42:14), and remembers his people like a nursing mother who remembers her baby at her breast (49:15).

We likewise see this combination of global salvation and personal intimacy in Jesus. Jesus is the one who brings a kind of light that honors the covenant God made with his people (42:6). This light gives freedom to those experiencing captivity (42:7)

and draws nations and kings out of their darkness to Jesus' light (60:2–3).

Jesus' light also provides personal and specific hope to those who have been sitting in dark dungeons awaiting their release and to those experiencing blindness (42:7). This light both shines across vast expanses around the world and peeks into the smallest crannies of our individual homes. This is the Jesus we await during Advent: the gleaming light illuminating and encouraging those all around the globe, and the candle glowing in each of our lives, reminding us of God's nearness.

Ponder Isaiah 42:1-14; 49:1-15; and 60:1-3.

How do you see the global nature of God's light in these passages? Where do you see its intimacy? How do you see both in Jesus?

The Light Leading Us Home

JAY Y. KIM

I am the light of the world. Whoever follows me will never walk in darkness, but will have the light of life.

JOHN 8:12

T he 19th-century English painter J. M. W. Turner was renowned for his stunning use of light. Stare long enough at pieces like *Snow Storm, Frosty Morning,* and—my personal favorite—*Fishermen at Sea,* and one gets the sense that Turner was painting with fire as much as oil and watercolors. Pastor and artist Michael Milton notes, "In Turner there is not merely light, but light leading the viewer in search of meaning." In the artwork of this master, light is not the end—it is an invitation toward hope, beauty, and meaning itself.

Walking around our neighborhood on cold evenings during the

Advent season, we are dazzled by arrays of Christmas lights. In recent years, seeing them through the eyes of my two young children has awakened something in me I'd lost to the subtle and insidious cynicism that often sets in with age: longing. Light is a wonderment because of its promise that there's something brilliant veiled behind the darkness, waiting to be found, pulsing with life, on the brink of unfolding before us.

In John 8:12, "when Jesus spoke again to the people, he said, 'I am the light of the world. Whoever follows me will never walk in darkness, but will have the light of life.'" The words alone are poetic enough, but this wasn't just a catchy metaphor. In announcing himself to be the Light of the World, in this particular place and at this particular time, Jesus was making a bold and beautiful declaration about what's veiled behind the darkness—and more importantly, about his own ability and willingness to get us there.

Jesus spoke these words during the Feast of Tabernacles, a weeklong Jewish festival centered on celebrating the Exodus, when God led his people out of slavery in Egypt and into freedom in the Promised Land. During their long journey through the wilderness, Yahweh had revealed himself to the people as a pillar of cloud by day and a pillar of fire by night (Ex. 13:21–22; 40:38). To remember this act of divine guidance during the Feast of Tabernacles, in the temple courts flames were lit atop two 75-foot-tall pillars to symbolize the pillar of light in Exodus. It is in this very setting that Jesus stands in the temple courts—likely in the light of these pillars—and declares, "I am the light of the world."

Jesus is the light guiding us through the wilderness of our despair, our pain, our loss. He is the light undoing the darkness of our fear, our anxiety, our uncertainty. He is the great Light of the World, leading us home.

Reflect on John 8:12.
Optional: Also read
John 9:5 and 12:46.

———————————

What do you imagine Jesus' first hearers thought or wondered when Jesus said this? How does the context of the Feast of Tabernacles enrich your understanding of his claim?

A Frightening and Freeing Light

JAY Y. KIM

Whoever lives by the truth comes into the light, so that it may be seen plainly that what they have done has been done in the sight of God.

JOHN 3:21

F or God so loved the world that he..."

Chances are, you can finish the line without a second thought. John 3:16 is arguably the most famous verse in the Bible—but it doesn't stand alone. Though the rest of the passage in this third chapter of John's gospel receives far less fanfare, it offers us a sobering and hopeful truth:

Light has come into the world, but people loved darkness instead of light.... But whoever lives by the truth comes into the light, so that it may be seen plainly that what they have done has been done in the sight of God. (vv. 19, 21)

Human experience is the paradoxical commingling of the love of darkness and the need for light. And this reality isn't just true *out there*, among

the sinful masses. This is true *right here*—in my heart, mind, and soul, and in yours. The apostle Paul aptly describes this pervasive and universal tension: "I do not understand what I do. For what I want to do I do not do, but what I hate I do" (Rom. 7:15). We've all been there. We still are.

Light can both expose and illuminate, making it simultaneously frightening and freeing. American physicist Richard Feynman said, "The first principle is that you must not fool yourself—and you are the easiest person to fool." If he was right—and I believe he was—then this frightening and freeing light is *exactly* what we need. This light exposes our pride and illuminates our shame, which have both stricken us since the very beginning of the human story.

In the Genesis creation narrative, God created a good world and placed Adam and Eve at its center, as his image-bearers, called to bring the earth's good potential to bear. But when the first humans sinned against God, it was because they came to believe the lie that they could be "like God" (Gen. 3:5). This is pride. And where does pride inevitably lead? Straight toward shame. "I was afraid because I was naked; so I hid," the man said (3:10).

Jesus, the Light, has come to free us from the darkness of pride and shame. The light has come to tell us the truth—that we are forgiven, accepted, loved. The light has come to undo the catastrophe of the Fall and to enact God's good new world, where we can all belong.

Meditate on John 3:16–21.

How is God's light frightening? How is it freeing? In what ways does the broader context of verse 16 deepen your understanding of Jesus' identity and purpose?

Delivered from Darkness

KRISTIE ANYABWILE

You are a chosen people . . . that you may declare the praises of him who called you out of darkness into his wonderful light.

1 PETER 2:9

It's a natural instinct to fear the dark. We know that bad things happen under cover of darkness. The same is true of spiritual darkness. Scripture tells us that the domain of darkness is where fruitless deeds reside and where ungodliness and evil dwell (Eph. 5:8–12). If we're under the control of darkness, we have no fellowship with God (1 John 1:5–7).

But Jesus came to deliver those blinded by darkness—to deliver us! Now, as people who dwell in the light of Christ, we strive to walk in a manner suitable for those who follow Jesus. We walk worshipfully, giving thanks for the great inheritance we have as coheirs with Christ.

In the beginning, God declared, "Let there be light," bringing day into existence (Gen. 1:3). God also declares, "Let there be light" in our own lives, referring not to the cosmos but to the

light of the gospel in our hearts that enables us to see the glory of Christ (2 Cor. 4:6). The Light of the World himself stepped down into the darkness of this world, into the darkness of our hearts, and opened our eyes so that we could declare the praises of him who called us out of darkness and into his wonderful light. In that light, there is righteousness, peace, and joy.

As citizens of Christ's kingdom of light, we have redemption, forgiveness, and fellowship with God. He made us—who once relished the darkness—his treasured possession.

God chose a people who would be his very own and reflect his holy character. He chose a people who would both embrace and transcend ethnic distinctions, declaring his praises within the beautiful diversity of his family. He chose a people to whom he would give the full privileges and blessings of the priesthood of believers—that is, direct access to God's very presence. The veil that once prohibited us from drawing near to God was torn so that "a new and living way" would open to us through Christ (Heb. 10:20). He chose a people whom he would welcome in his presence at all times—a people who would declare his praises as we offer individual and corporate spiritual sacrifices to God.

This Advent season, we celebrate the Promised One who delivered us from darkness, who called us into his wonderful light so that we might bask in the Son and declare his praises.

Contemplate Colossians 1:9–14 and 1 Peter 2:9.

What does it mean for you to live as part of the kingdom of light? How has Jesus, the Light, brought you understanding and purpose?

Christ in Ten Thousand Places

MARLENA GRAVES

*For God, who said,
"Let light shine out
of darkness," made
his light shine in
our hearts to give
us the light of the
knowledge of God's
glory displayed in
the face of Christ.*
2 CORINTHIANS 4:6

I n Plato's famous Allegory of the Cave, people live imprisoned in chains, staring ahead at a wall with a fire casting light from behind them. Unbeknownst to them, puppets and moving objects behind them are creating the shadows they see on the wall. They believe the shadows are reality. They have no idea that there is a bright sunlit world outside. Even when others tell them about the real world, they still don't want to leave their cave.

The allegory reminds me of Paul's words: "The god of this age has blinded the minds of unbelievers, so that they cannot see the light of the gospel that displays the glory of Christ, who is the image of God" (2 Cor. 4:4). In contrast, when we are born anew in Christ, we become children of the light—children of the sunlit world (Eph. 5:8). God illuminates our hearts and minds through the gospel so we can see Christ in his glory. As we fix our eyes on Jesus and remain in him, God progressively puts everything in its proper perspective. The result is that the church collectively and people individually are better able to discern good from evil. We grow to see and discern the details of beauty, goodness, and truth—to see the world and people aright. No doubt, we need each other to remain in the light to experience God's shalom—to see and to love.

Ephesians 5:9 reveals something breathtakingly beautiful about the fruit born of light. The fruit is "all goodness, righteousness and truth." Gazing at the face of Christ, we start to see him more and more in our lives and in our world. We see Jesus showing up in thousands of ways and in all sorts of places—sometimes quite unexpectedly. We're enabled to find the goodness, righteousness, and truth present even in difficult or painful circumstances. Similarly, others see these virtues manifested in our own lives and give thanks to God.

The knowledge revealed to us through God enlightening our hearts fills us with overflowing joy and enduring hope (Eph. 1:18). It is hope for the present because of the "incomparably great power" we have through the Spirit to do God's will in the world (v. 19). This hope is further buttressed by the knowledge that God is ever for us. And we also have hope for the future because we catch glimpses of our glorious inheritance.

Indeed, as we remain in Christ and connected to one another, we know at a deep level that evil is the counterfeit, the shadow world. As Gerard Manley Hopkins described in his poem "As Kingfishers Catch Fire," we grow to see Christ playing "in ten thousand places" and the glory of God shining everywhere. This is Advent light.

Consider 2 Corinthians 4:4-6 and Ephesians 1:15-23; 5:8-11.

How do these passages describe what spiritual illumination looks like? How has faith in Jesus—the Light—enlightened your own life?

He Shines in the Darkness

CAROLYN ARENDS

T he apostle John contextualizes his account of the words and deeds of his good friend Jesus with an opening prologue that crackles with energy and wonder. Jesus, John wants to tell us, is the very Word of God. He was with God at the creation of the world. He *is* God. He is life itself, and that life is the light of the world.

Then comes verse 5: "The light shines in the darkness, and the darkness has not overcome it." At least that's what it says in my 2011 edition of the NIV. But here's a striking thing: My older edition of the NIV (the 1984 translation) reads differently. It says, "The light shines in the darkness, but the darkness has not understood it."

The Greek word alternatively rendered "overcome" and "understood" is *katalambanó*—which means to "take hold of" or "grasp." We need more than one English word to try to hint at the full gist of what John is saying here.

John has seen the Light of the World with his own eyes. He's gone fishing with him. He's eaten with him. He's prayed with him. And he's watched him endure the most horrific death imaginable and then *come back to life*. So John knows that there is no darkness in the universe that can permanently grasp and defeat this light. The darkness cannot *overcome* it.

But John also knows that our human minds, left to their own

*The Word became
flesh and made his
dwelling among us.*

JOHN 1:14

devices, cannot begin to grasp the love on offer in the astonishing fact of the Incarnation. The darkness cannot *understand* it.

John's prologue culminates with a breathtaking meditation on the lengths to which God has gone to reach us with his illuminating love. "The Word became flesh," he writes, "and made his dwelling among us." Or, as *The Message* paraphrase renders it, the flesh-and-blood Word "moved into the neighborhood."

The Mighty God came in the staggeringly vulnerable form of a human baby. The Prince of Peace allowed himself to be birthed into a world of sin and chaos—God made huggable, woundable, kissable, killable.

Only the Light of the World can give us the power to begin to understand what God has offered us in the birth of Jesus. So, this Advent, let us pray the prayer the apostle Paul offered the Ephesians (3:18): that we, "being rooted and established in love, may have power, together with all the Lord's holy people, to grasp how wide and long and high and deep is the love of Christ."

Ponder John 1:1-18.

What does this passage emphasize about the about the Word? About Jesus as the Light of the World? About the Incarnation? What questions, thoughts, or feelings does it stir up in you? Express your response to God in prayer.

Immanuel

As we journey through the events surrounding the Nativity,
we contemplate the Incarnation. Jesus—the Mighty
God, the Prince of Peace, the Light of the World—
became flesh and dwelt among us. As Isaiah's prophecy
foretold, he is "God with us." Jesus is Immanuel.

Waiting On a Promise

DORENA WILLIAMSON

Do not be afraid, Zechariah; your prayer has been heard. Your wife Elizabeth will bear you a son, and you are to call him John.

LUKE 1:13

T he Old Testament concludes with a promise of one who would reconcile the hearts of fathers to their children. Those words ending the book of Malachi echoed over centuries of silence. In the period of waiting between the Old and New Testaments, our Mighty God was setting up the tumultuous world stage for the coming of the Prince of Peace.

There is a time for everything, and Luke 1 is an intricate tapestry of divine appointments. The setting was an appointed time in history: during the reign of Herod. Zechariah was appointed for a once-in-a-lifetime priestly duty. Elizabeth's long years of infertility were an appointed impossible situation that set up the miraculous conception of John the Baptist. The couple's priestly lineage was an appointed heritage for raising an anointed son. And Gabriel was the appointed messenger to announce God's appointed purpose for John the Baptist.

When they were young and starting out their life together, Zechariah and Elizabeth were likely full of hopeful expectations about their future. But as infertile months turned into years, the hope of having a child ebbed away and felt like a burden of "disgrace" (Luke 1:25).

When we're introduced to this couple, they're now "very old" yet are continuing to walk with God. This *faithfulness* deserves our commendation—rather than criticism of Zechariah's moment of unbelief. After all, this aged man had grown so familiar with disappointment.

Zechariah had persevered in prayer through seemingly dark and silent years. But on this day, as he performed the priestly duty of lighting the fire to burn incense, Gabriel appeared and announced that God had heard his prayer. God was *with* Zechariah—even when heaven seemed silent. The Light of the World had not forgotten; he was sovereignly preparing history for the appointed time.

Zechariah and Elizabeth's story offers us perspective on our own seasons of waiting. We're reminded that there's no expiration date on our prayers. The faithfulness of this couple unfolded into a life-giving season of joy as God's promise came to fulfillment through their child, the forerunner of the Messiah.

But as we enter into their story, there is also no skipping over their decades of infertility. We enter into this painful part of their lives too. For in their long sorrow, we see their strong faith.

Elizabeth understood that in this miracle, God had shown her special favor. Many biblical heroes did not receive what they hoped for or what had been promised them this side of eternity (Heb. 11:39). The ultimate fulfillment of their faith was beyond them—as it also is for us. This Advent, in our waiting, there is a bigger picture being painted—in God's appointed time. Immanuel—God with us—is still faithful to his promises today.

Reflect on Luke 1:5-25.

How do you see faithfulness in this story? Zechariah and Elizabeth's faithfulness? God's? How do you see God's sovereignty? God's presence?

Read Luke 1:26-38

The Beautiful Paradox

KELLY M. KAPIC

You will conceive and give birth to a son, and you are to call him Jesus. He will be great and will be called the Son of the Most High.

LUKE 1:31-32

The abstract concept of *power* brings to mind earthquakes and thunderstorms or maybe presidents and billionaires. Raw power stops us in our tracks, causing us to give heed to whatever or whoever wields it. Few of us, however, associate power with the womb. Yet Mary's womb carried true power, hidden in darkness, unseen, hard to imagine.

Here we encounter one of the most beautiful paradoxes of the Christian faith: The Holy Spirit brought into being a tiny baby boy in this woman's womb, her own flesh and bone, her firstborn son; this same baby boy was none other than the Son of God, identified as the "Son of the Most High."

So is Jesus Mary's son or God's Son? Human or divine? Yes! Both are true in one person, this one baby boy. We can imagine God bringing salvation, or we can picture a heroic human doing revolutionary things. But a single person

who is at the same time both fully God and fully human, without compromising the integrity of either? This is truly a beautiful paradox—a paradox at the heart of human salvation.

This power is not a bare, infinite force abstracted from all other definition but the compassion of the eternal, glorious, holy God clothed in human flesh. His power takes the form of weakness in divine solidarity with humankind, all driven by his holy love.

The angel proclaimed a glorious event to Mary—and to us. Jesus gets his full humanity from Mary, becoming like the rest of us in all ways except that he refuses sin (Heb. 4:15). Yet Mary's son existed *before* Mary, for this is the eternal Son of God who, as the Nicene Creed declares, is "very God of very God." Having the eternal nature of God, the Son comes by the Spirit from the Father, never ceasing to be the Mighty God yet truly becoming what he was

not: a humble human creature. Jesus—truly God and truly human.

As Leo I (400–461) wrote in a letter, commenting on the Son's incarnation, "What he did was to enhance humanity not diminish deity. That self-emptying of his, by which the invisible revealed himself visible and the Creator and Lord of all things elected to be reckoned among mortals, was a drawing-near in mercy not a failure in power." From the womb of Mary comes the savior-king, whose "kingdom will never end." May we, like Mary, respond as the "Lord's servant," willing to trust the Almighty God who has loved his creation enough to dwell in it by becoming this man, thus bringing new life into the world. His full divinity and full humanity proclaim his power, and he tells us, "Do not be afraid."

Consider Luke 1:26–38.

What strikes you most in Gabriel's message? How do you desire to respond to Jesus and to the beautiful paradox of his incarnation?

The Invitation of Incarnation

RASOOL BERRY

Blessed is she who has believed that the Lord would fulfill his promises to her!

LUKE 1:45

F ew interruptions in life are as disruptive as travel, especially with the fatigue and morning sickness that often accompany early pregnancy. Mary's journey from Nazareth to the hills of Judea was neither easy nor safe. Still, emboldened by her faith but also in need of support, Mary braved the trek pregnant, poor, and probably perplexed. Why choose to go at all?

Gabriel had told Mary that her relative Elizabeth was also expecting a child—a miracle for a woman of her advanced age. Recognizing that Elizabeth was the only person on earth who might understand what she was going through, Mary went to her. And when she arrived, Elizabeth offered the exact affirmation Mary needed: "Blessed are you among women, and blessed is the child you will bear!" Elizabeth praised Mary for her response of faith. With those words, I imagine Mary's fears tied to her unexpected pregnancy and its unknown consequences for her life faded into greater faith.

Elizabeth's encouragement reminded Mary that the Lord's interruption of her plans was also an invitation—not only to carry and give birth to Immanuel, "God with us," but also to engage in a deeper sense of community, "us with us." Heartened by Elizabeth's blessing, Mary responded with a song of praise. And she reflected on this invitation into interdependence in the closing words of her Magnificat: "He has helped his servant Israel, in remembrance of his mercy, as he spoke to our fathers, to Abraham and to his offspring forever" (ESV). In her rejoicing, Mary meditated on how the very same God who "spoke to our fathers" all the way back to Abraham had now spoken to her and to Elizabeth.

Mary believed in "God with us," and she said yes when Gabriel appeared to her. But her faith still needed nurturing. The Incarnation meant a major interruption in Mary's life; it was wonderful, yes, but it was also weighty. Something was happening to her that had never happened before in the history of the world, and she needed support and help to accept and prepare for it.

So she turned to faithful Elizabeth. We can only imagine how strengthening it was for Mary to hear Elizabeth's words of blessing. In fact, I'd argue that we would not have Mary's Magnificat without Elizabeth's Encouragement.

That's the power of interdependence, of faith in community. In our individualistic society, opening ourselves up to be blessed by others is often difficult. We are conditioned to consider the possibilities of harm more than the potential helpfulness of community. But the truth is that, like Mary, we all need Elizabeth-like encouragement. The Incarnation is an interruption and an invitation to know "God with us" and also to embrace "us with us."

Contemplate Luke 1:39–56.

What truths do you see in this passage about Jesus— God with us? How do Elizabeth's words and her role in Mary's life speak to you, too, about the "us with us" nature of faith?

Read Luke 1:57–80

God of Mercy and Power

MADISON N. PIERCE

*Praise be to the
Lord, the God of
Israel, because he has
come to his people
and redeemed them.*

LUKE 1:68

W e humans do not hold mercy and power in tension well. Those who gain power often enjoy it and tend to seek more, while those who are gracious tend to surrender power (or have it taken from them). Undoubtedly there are exceptions, but by and large, we know and can observe that this balance is not easy to achieve. But unlike us, God is somehow *both* the most powerful and the most merciful, perfect in his display of each.

We see God's gracious might highlighted in several ways in this story about John the Baptist's birth and early days. In fact, this theme of gracious might is hidden in plain sight for us English readers. We learn that Elizabeth wants to name the boy John in keeping with the message that Gabriel gave to Zechariah (Luke 1:13). Those around her are surprised; this didn't cohere with the custom of naming a child after someone in the family. So

why John (*Yohanan* in Hebrew)? It means "God is gracious," and this boy will proclaim God's gracious works on behalf of the whole world.

Zechariah has been unable to speak since the day he learned his wife would have a child. But as soon as he writes the boy's name, his speech is restored, and he erupts in praise. Through this sign, the people know this boy is special. They ask one another, *What will he be?*

But Zechariah casts their gaze in the right direction. Yes, the boy has a special role, but *the Lord* is to be praised. The powerful Lord of all "will come to us," Zechariah says, and will be in the midst of his people.

But the Lord's display of power will not be oppressive. Instead, it will be liberative. The Lord has "raised up a horn of salvation" in order to "show mercy to our ancestors" and to "rescue us."

The idea of God showing mercy is linked to the idea of God's people being in sin. Like their ancestors who received similar prophecies (1 Sam. 2:10; Mic. 7:20; Ezek. 16:60), they deserve punishment but they receive an outpouring of grace.

Why does God do this? So we can serve him. This is a gift so that we might truly experience "God with us." The Song of Zechariah promises forgiveness of our sins and illumination to guide us on the "path of peace." As Luke continues his gospel, he will return to these themes many times, highlighting how the coming of the Messiah ushers in restoration and justice—true and lasting peace.

Meditate on Luke 1:57-80.

Where in this passage do you see the mighty power of God? Where do you see the mercy and grace of God? Pray, expressing your response to God.

Unfather Christmas

J. D. PEABODY

*And he gave him
the name Jesus.*

MATTHEW 1:25

J oseph's biggest claim to fame is who he wasn't. We know him as "not the real dad" of Jesus. Matthew emphasizes how little Joseph had to do with the unfolding redemption story, from Mary's pregnancy to the location of Christ's birth to the events that led to the family's flight into Egypt.

Scripture also renders Joseph conspicuously silent. He utters not one recorded word. As a result, Joseph is often either glossed over or is the subject of our conjecture. We want to know more. Yet perhaps Joseph's non-contribution is the very thing God would have us remember.

This man's most significant role is his apparent lack of one. His diminished involvement encapsulates a central tenet of the gospel: Salvation belongs to God alone. Joseph's story reminds us we are not the orchestrators of our own rescue. The angel didn't tell Joseph, "Here's what God wants, so now go make it happen." He said, essentially, "Here's what *God* has made happen, and here's how to receive that truth."

It would have been understandable for Joseph to resent life not unfolding as he'd expected. But rather than focus on all he was being asked to give up, Joseph made room for a greater reality: This child was the Promised One, the key to God's redemption of the whole world. And if Jesus was truly good news for all people, that included him. The bigger plan for humanity also meant salvation for him personally.

So it's worth noting that Joseph's silence is broken with a single word. He's not quoted directly, but we're told he spoke it, and the word was *Jesus*. Joseph alone had the honor of giving the child a name that means "God saves."

Matthew links this name with the text in Isaiah identifying the Messiah as Immanuel—God with us. *Jesus* and *Immanuel* are virtually interchangeable names; God's presence makes our salvation possible, and our salvation allows us to stand in his presence.

For Joseph, assigning this name was more than following the angel's orders. It was a declaration. The man who says nothing speaks loudly here. In his helplessness, when his world went sideways, Joseph's response was *Jesus. God saves.*

As events unfolded over which he had little control, Joseph could personalize the words of the prophet: *Immanuel. God is with me.* And when he would soon face such peril that he and his family would have to run for their lives, Joseph carried the truth in his arms. Jesus. God saves. Immanuel. God goes with us.

Though the space allotted to Joseph in the narrative is small, maybe that's a good thing. In Joseph, we can see our own smallness and remember that salvation belongs to the Savior who is with us to the end.

Reflect on Matthew 1:18–25.

How does Joseph's act of naming Jesus speak to you? What do you imagine this name meant to Joseph as he took care of the infant Jesus?

A Flock of Shepherds

J. D. PEABODY

*And there were
shepherds living out
in the fields nearby,
keeping watch over
their flocks at night.*

LUKE 2:8

W hen my wife, Karin, was in preschool, she played a miniature Mary in a living Nativity scene. While it was an adorable idea, the reality of having live animals stand next to a three-year-old proved terrifying for her. She cried hysterically, wanting no part of the whole thing. To console her, her father stepped into the scene and lay down on the ground between her and the beasts, forming a human barricade so that his daughter felt secure. He covered himself entirely with straw so visitors to the living Nativity were none the wiser.

It's a striking image of what shepherding is all about. In Luke 2, the shepherds are "keeping watch over their flocks at night"—highlighting the very real dangers of darkness. It was when thieves and predators posed the greatest threat. So the shepherds placed themselves in harm's way, protecting their sheep with their very lives.

But in Luke's account of Jesus' birth, the shepherds also turn out to be sheep. That first Christmas, the Lord revealed himself as the Good Shepherd in the story, caring for the shepherds themselves as part of his own flock.

Consider how much God's attention to the shepherds resembles David's description of God as a shepherd in Psalm 23. God supplied the shepherds' need—a need they may not have even articulated. He quieted their souls through the angel's words: "Do not be afraid." He led them on paths of righteousness straight to the manger. He showed he was with them in the most humble and relatable of ways: as a baby in a manger. He restored their souls with a message of hope and belonging—a message that turned out exactly "as they had been told." He filled their cup to overflowing with praise "for all the things they had heard and seen." He not only met their need; he anointed their heads with the oil of joy. He showed them goodness and mercy that would no doubt stay with them all the days of their life.

I need that kind of care. As a pastor, I'm grateful for this reminder that shepherds are also part of the flock. I'm thankful for a Savior who knows his skittish sheep well, who laid his life all the way down in the hay, placing himself between us and every danger.

And I'm grateful that when our anxious souls need tending, the Lord still speaks the word of peace on earth in the recognizable voice of our Good Shepherd. That is indeed good news of great joy for all the people.

Contemplate Luke 2:1–21.
*Optional: Also read Psalm 23
and John 10:2–4, 11, 14.*

How do you see God's care—
and God's character—in the
account of the shepherds?
What does this emphasize
for you about Jesus?

Seeing Jesus, They Knew

KRISTIE ANYABWILE

P arenting is hard, and first-time parenting brings an added weight of difficulty. Everything is new—from feeling those first flutters of life in the womb to holding and seeing your child for the first time to the first bath, first feedings, first words, first steps. There are so many *firsts*!

Imagine what it was like for Joseph and Mary, traveling with their newborn from Bethlehem to Jerusalem. The trip would've taken a few hours on foot. In faithful obedience, they traveled for the first time as brand-new parents, participating in the custom of dedicating themselves and their child back to God.

All went according to custom until the righteous and devout Simeon arrived. He'd been waiting for the deliverance of Israel, and entering the temple courts, he experienced a first. In that moment, God fulfilled his promise that Simeon would live to see the Messiah. Seeing the infant Jesus, he *knew*.

And Simeon didn't just see him—Simeon *held* him. In that moment, Simeon tangibly understood that God's salvation foretold by the prophets would be not only global in scale but also intimate and personal. Salvation itself was embodied in the cooing and wiggling infant in his arms. As Simeon worshiped and spoke of God's salvation, Mary and Joseph marveled, likely remembering the angels' instruction that they should name their child Jesus, a name that spoke of God's salvation.

*For my eyes have seen
your salvation, which
you have prepared in
the sight of all nations.*

LUKE 2:30-31

While Simeon spoke to Mary, Anna came up to them and confirmed Simeon's prophetic song of worship by praising God herself. For decades, Anna's entire life had centered on worshiping God, praying, and fasting. Seeing Jesus, Anna *knew*. She knew this was the child they'd been awaiting for the redemption of God's people, so she spoke of Jesus to all who would listen. The promised light for the nations had arrived.

In Mary and Joseph, in Simeon and Anna, we see snapshots of what devotion to God and righteous living looks like. We see obedience and faith, discipline and dedication, anticipation and worship. They saw Immanuel. They held Immanuel. They knew Immanuel. They spoke of Immanuel.

As we celebrate Immanuel this Advent, let's walk in faithful obedience like Mary and Joseph. Let's practice being devoted, upright, and worshipful like Simeon. Let's pray, fast, and speak of Jesus to all who will hear like Anna. There is redemption in no other name.

Ponder Luke 2:22-40.

What's most compelling to you about the stories of Simeon and Anna? How does their example—and that of Mary and Joseph—encourage and inspire you this Christmas Eve?

CHRISTMAS DAY

For to us a child is born, to us a son is given, and the government will be on his shoulders. And he will be called Wonderful Counselor, Mighty God, Everlasting Father, Prince of Peace. Of the greatness of his government and peace there will be no end. He will reign on David's throne and over his kingdom, establishing and upholding it with justice and righteousness from that time on and forever.

ISAIAH 9:6–7

Read Isaiah 7:14 and 9:1-7   *Celebrate* Jesus' birth with joy.
→

Light of the World, Hope of the Nations

RASOOL BERRY

T hroughout history, humans have looked up to the night sky to search for signs from above. That proclivity has led many to worship the stars and celestial bodies. In Genesis 1, the terms *sun* and *moon* are not used; they are instead described as the greater and lesser lights (v. 16), likely to avoid the names commonly evoked in idol worship in the ancient Near East.

Yet God would soon use that same human search for signs in the stars to reveal his covenant: He commanded Abraham to look up and witness the

When they saw the star, they were overjoyed. On coming to the house, they saw the child . . . and they bowed down and worshiped him.

MATTHEW 2:10-11

innumerable stars, foreshadowing the blessing of his progeny to the nations. Hundreds of years later, however, when the children of Abraham were exiled to Babylon, it appeared that the darkness of the nations had devoured the light. Hope appeared to be lost.

But in Matthew 2, we find an unexpected redemptive reversal! We meet the Magi—from an elite class known for astrology (and idolatry) and likely from the same region where God's people had been exiled—whose study of the skies led them to faith in the promise of Abraham. *Had the stories passed down from Daniel and the exiles in Babylon finally come to pass?* Likely venturing on the same 900-mile journey from ancient Babylon to Jerusalem that the returning exiles had made so many years before, the Magi sought an answer to a single question: "Where is the one who has been born king of the Jews?"

Their inquiry revealed a deep spiritual yearning: "We saw his star . . . and have come to worship him." Their journey was a fulfillment of Isaiah's prophetic vision and a foretaste of what was to come: "I will make you as a light for the nations, that my salvation may reach to the end of the earth" (49:6, ESV). The "lesser light" of the star pointed the Magi to the "greater light" in the little town of Bethlehem, bright enough to enlighten the nations. The light came into the world, and the darkness did not conquer it.

The light of the Epiphany—the appearance of God in the arrival of Jesus—continues to offer hope to all nations groping in the dark for divine truth. And as the Magi show us, this is news too good to keep to ourselves! These wise men from the East continue to teach us that we too must travel far and wide to share the news that Jesus is the Light of the World and the hope of the nations. As Scripture tells us: "You are a chosen people, a royal priesthood, a holy nation, God's special possession, that you may declare the praises of him who called you out of darkness into his wonderful light" (1 Pet. 2:9).

Reflect on Matthew 2:1-12 and Isaiah 49:6; 60:3.

What does the visit of the Magi reveal about Jesus' identity and purpose? How is the Spirit prompting you to respond to Jesus, the Light of the World?

ALICIA AKINS is a graduate student in biblical studies at Reformed Theological Seminary in Washington, DC, and the author of *Invitations to Abundance.*

KRISTIE ANYABWILE is the author of *Literarily: How Understanding Bible Genres Transforms Bible Study* and the editor of *His Testimonies, My Heritage.*

CAROLYN ARENDS is a recording artist, an author, and the director of education for Renovaré. Her most recent album is *In the Morning.*

RASOOL BERRY serves as teaching pastor at The Bridge Church in Brooklyn, New York. He is also the host of the *Where Ya From?* podcast.

CRAIG L. BLOMBERG is distinguished professor emeritus of New Testament at Denver Seminary and the author of numerous books, including his *Matthew* commentary and *Interpreting the Parables.*

MARLENA GRAVES is professor of spiritual formation at Northeastern Seminary. She is the author of several books, including *The Way Up Is Down.*

KELLY M. KAPIC is a theologian at Covenant College and the author or editor of numerous books, including *Embodied Hope* and *You're Only Human.*

JAY Y. KIM serves as lead pastor at WestGate Church. He's the author of *Analog Church* and *Analog Christian* and lives in Silicon Valley with his family.

GLENN PACKIAM is the lead pastor of Rockharbor Church in Costa Mesa, California. He's the author of *The Resilient Pastor* and coauthor of *The Intentional Year*.

J. D. PEABODY pastors New Day Church in Federal Way, Washington, and is the author of *Perfectly Suited: The Armor of God for the Anxious Mind*.

MADISON N. PIERCE is associate professor of New Testament at Western Theological Seminary. Her books include *Divine Discourse in the Epistle to the Hebrews*.

ADRIEL SANCHEZ is pastor of North Park Presbyterian Church in San Diego and the host of *Core Christianity*, a Q&A radio broadcast and podcast.

SARAH SHIN is a doctoral student in systematic theology at the University of Aberdeen, Scotland. She is the author of *Beyond Colorblind: Redeeming Our Ethnic Journey*.

BETH STOVELL teaches Old Testament at Ambrose Seminary. She is the coeditor of *Theodicy and Hope in the Book of the Twelve* and the author of the forthcoming commentaries *Minor Prophets I* and *II*.

JEREMY TREAT is a pastor at Reality LA and an adjunct professor at Biola University. He is the author of *Seek First* and *The Crucified King*.

DORENA WILLIAMSON is a church planter, speaker, and the author of *ColorFull, The Celebration Place, Crowned with Glory*, and *Brown Baby Jesus*.

Ideas for Families

THROUGHOUT ADVENT

- With teens or preteens, read and discuss the devotions together each evening. With younger kids, focus on just the Scripture passages and reflection prompts.

- Begin a family journal for Advent. At the top of each page, write, "Jesus is . . . " After reading and discussing the day's passage, invite family members to write a phrase or sentence or doodle an image to record their ideas about Jesus.

ANY TIME DURING ADVENT

- Put a simple puzzle together as a family *without* using a picture of the puzzle's completed image. Afterward, discuss how seeing parts of the puzzle come together helped you see the big picture more clearly. Discuss how the Bible's promises help us develop a fuller picture of who Jesus is.

- Play Who Am I? (also called 20 Questions) as a family. Discuss how the more we learn, the easier it is to identify or recognize someone. Talk about how Scripture's promises about Jesus help us understand his identity.

WEEK 1: MIGHTY GOD

- Look together at baby pictures of each family member. Discuss the limitations and abilities of a human newborn. Explore how amazing it is that Jesus—the Mighty God—was born as a human infant.

- Use Legos, building blocks, or other craft supplies to create a castle. Talk together about the eternal kingdom and reign of God using ideas in Revelation 21:1–4.

WEEK 2: PRINCE OF PEACE

- Create placemats to use during Advent by coloring maps of the world. Discuss the idea that Jesus' peace and the salvation he offers are for the whole world—for people of all nations, languages, and cultures.

- Invite everyone to name injustices, wrongs, sorrows, fears, or instances of violence in the world today that they long for Jesus to put right. Write them on pieces of construction paper. Together, tear those papers up, then glue the pieces together (text side down) in the shape of a cross to represent the ultimate peace Jesus will bring.

WEEK 3: LIGHT OF THE WORLD

- Go stargazing or look online at pictures from NASA's James Webb Space Telescope. Discuss how light breaks through darkness—and how Jesus is like a light to us, shining even during dark times.

- Talk together about sharing the light of Jesus with others. Purchase glowsticks together and create tags with a simple message your children want to share, like "Jesus is the Light of the World. Jesus loves you!" Then walk or drive to nearby homes to give them to friends and neighbors.

WEEK 4: IMMANUEL

- As you walk through the stories and experiences of people in the Nativity, bring their experiences to life by discussing these questions together: What do you imagine this person felt, thought, or wondered? How do you imagine you'd react if you were in their place? Why?

- Make simple yarn or bead bracelets together and wear them daily during the week. Encourage your kids to remember this truth every time they see it: *God is with us*, right here, right now.

Ideas for Groups

THROUGHOUT ADVENT

• To use this resource with your Bible study group, encourage members to read the daily Scripture passages, devotions, and reflection prompts. When you gather, select several of the week's Scripture passages and reflection questions to guide your discussion.

• Print out the libretto of Handel's *Messiah*. Select portions to read aloud and listen to parts of the music that emphasize the week's theme.

WEEK 1: MIGHTY GOD

• Play an identity game: Have everyone anonymously write down a little-known fact about themselves. Collect and read the answers, then take turns guessing who said what. Keep going until everyone has been guessed. Discuss the goal of coming to know Jesus—whom you already know and love—even more deeply during Advent.

WEEK 2: PRINCE OF PEACE

• Compare and contrast our common, often-limited understanding of peace with the expansive vision of shalom in Isaiah's promises and other parts of Scripture. Optional: Create a collage together by writing words and pasting images from magazines onto a posterboard to represent the holistic nature of shalom.

WEEK 3: LIGHT OF THE WORLD

• Darken the room, then have each person light a candle as you each read aloud a key passage or verse from this week's assigned Scripture passages. As you read and listen, focus on prayerfully contemplating Jesus' identity as the Light of the World.

WEEK 4: IMMANUEL

• Think through all the different people involved in the Nativity events, then invite everyone in the group to share who they relate to most and why. Prompt group members to focus primarily on how their spiritual journey may resonate with one of the scenes or experiences in Scripture.

Made in the USA
Las Vegas, NV
16 November 2022

59674678R00046